Classic Recipes of
MOROCCO

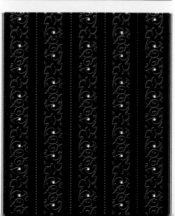

Classic Recipes of
MOROCCO

TRADITIONAL FOOD AND COOKING
IN 25 AUTHENTIC DISHES

GHILLIE BAŞAN

LORENZ BOOKS

This edition is published by Lorenz Books,
an imprint of Anness Publishing Ltd,
108 Great Russell Street,
London WC1B 3NA
info@anness.com
www.annesspublishing.com
twitter: @Anness_Books

© Anness Publishing Limited 2015

If you like the images in this book and
would like to investigate using them for
publishing, promotions or advertising,
please visit our website
www.practicalpictures.com for more
information.

Publisher: Joanna Lorenz
Editor: Helen Sudell
Designer: Nigel Partridge
Recipe Photography: Martin Brigdale
Food Stylist: Linda Tubby
Stylist: Helen Trent
Production Controller: Rosanna Anness

A CIP catalogue record for this book is
available from the British Library

PUBLISHER'S NOTE
Although the advice and information in this
book are believed to be accurate and true
at the time of going to press, neither the
authors nor the publisher can accept any
legal responsibility or liability for any errors
or omissions that may have been made nor
for any inaccuracies nor for any loss, harm
or injury that comes about from following
instructions or advice in this book.

PUBLISHER'S ACKNOWLEDGMENTS
The Publisher would like to thank the
following agencies for the use of their
images. Istock p6, 9, 11 (bottom).

Previously published as part of a larger
volume *Modern Moroccan*.

COOK'S NOTES
Bracketed terms are intended for American
readers. For all recipes, quantities are given
in both metric and imperial measures and,
where appropriate, in standard cups and
spoons. Follow one set of measures, but
not a mixture, because they are not
interchangeable.

Standard spoon and cup measures are
level. 1 tsp = 5ml, 1 tbsp = 15ml, 1 cup =
250ml/8fl oz. Australian standard
tablespoons are 20ml. Australian readers
should use 3 tsp in place of 1 tbsp for
measuring small quantities.

American pints are 16fl oz/2 cups.
American readers should use 20fl oz/2.5
cups in place of 1 pint when measuring
liquids.

Electric oven temperatures in this book are
for conventional ovens. When using a fan
oven, the temperature will probably need to
be reduced by about 10–20°C/20–40°F.
Since ovens vary, you should check with
your manufacturer's instruction book for
guidance.

The nutritional analysis given for each
recipe is calculated per portion (i.e. serving
or item), unless otherwise stated. If the
recipe gives a range, such as Serves 4–6,
then the nutritional analysis will be for the
smaller portion size, i.e. 6 servings. The
analysis does not include optional
ingredients, such as salt added to taste.

Medium (US large) eggs are used unless
otherwise stated.

Contents

Introduction

Morocco is a vast country of desert, rugged mountainous terrain, and fertile plains, with the Atlantic Ocean and Mediterranean sea lapping its shores. The influences of the past can clearly been seen in modern Moroccan cuisine – from the traditional foods that have been eaten for millenia to the contribution made by the different peoples from Africa, Arabia and Europe that have lived here, and the evolving trade that developed between continents. A writer once described Moroccan cuisine as 'the perfumed soul of our culture'; a unique blend of African, Arabian and European influences. The result is a cuisine characterized by its subtle scents, delicate flavours and elegant presentation.

Left: The ancient fortified city of Ait Benhaddou, situated along the former caravan route between the Sahara and Marrakech.

Culinary Influences

Moroccan food and cooking is a fascinating reflection of the history of a country whose invaders have come and gone, each leaving a stamp on the cuisine. Apart from the indigenous Berbers who lived in the fertile plains, Carthaginians, Romans and Vandals all invaded North Africa and ruled for several hundred years.

However, none of these empires was to have such an impact on the region and its culinary history as the new force rising in the East – the Arabs and Islam. They brought spices

Below: Street food is readily available throughout Morocco.

Above: A typical food trader in an outside food market, Fez.

from the East, rice from India, the Persian habit of combining meat and fruit in stews, the idea of the scented broth, and the tradition of mezze – a spread of appetizers.

Modern Morocco

Today, Morocco is a culinary haven. In the north, in cities such as Tangier and Tetouan, there is a Spanish influence in the language, architecture and food. In Fez, the senses are stimulated by hypnotizing aromas. This city has dominated Moroccan trade, culture and religious life since the end of the

tenth century and its cuisine is a unique reflection of the diversity of its inhabitants, which have included Berbers, Jews, Arabs, Andalusians, the French and other Europeans. Casablanca, the principal city of Morocco and the largest port in the Maghreb, is cosmopolitan in its food. Further south, in Marrakech, Safi, and Essaouira, the culinary influences come from Africa and the Atlantic.

Marrakech earned its place in the world as a vibrant market-place for the goods of Atlas tribes, Maghrebis from the plains, and nomads from the Sahara. It is particularly interesting for its Berber origins, which are reflected in the low, red buildings as well as the food. Inland though, in the harsher terrain of the Rif, the Atlas and the southern oases, there has been little outside influence and the nomadic Berber tribes still hold on to their ancient culinary identity.

Right: Dried fruit and nuts on sale in a market in Marrakech.

Moroccan Eating Traditions

Most meals begin with a simple selection of mezze, which might include a bowl of olives, a cooked vegetable salad dressed with olive oil, sprinkled with cumin and served with a dip, flat bread and a savoury pastry. The tagines or a roast meat dish may come next, often served with a punchy, fresh raw salad to soothe the palate. Couscous may follow but traditionally, when couscous is accompanied by a stew or broth, it is usually reserved for a meal on its own. A simple plate of fresh fruit or dessert marks the end of the meal before mint tea is served.

The room where the food is cooked displays none of the grandeur or exoticism of the actual dishes, as a traditional Moroccan kitchen is semi-dark, cool in the heat of summer and damp in winter. The cooking utensils are simple, either glazed earthenware tagines or copper pots. There is an old stove fired by charcoal, which blackens the tiled walls but cooks gently, and a portable kanoun, a brazier made of sun-baked clay.

Attending a diffa

When visiting the country, one of the most exciting ways of sampling a variety of dishes is to attend a feast, called a *diffa*. This may involve half a dozen dishes rising to as many as twenty courses for a special feast to celebrate a wedding. Traditionally, the guests sit on cushions around a low table. The first dish to be served is the impressive *bistilla*, a round, layered, paper-thin pastry enclosing two savoury fillings of stewed pigeon and

Above: Couscous can be a meal in itself.

spices, and one sweet filling of sautéed almonds with icing (confectioners') sugar and cinnamon. The bistilla is fried in butter on both sides, sprinkled with sugar and cinnamon in a decorative pattern, and served on a platter in the middle of the table.

The second dish of a diffa is usually a *choua*, a steamed shoulder of lamb flavoured with cumin or, in the countryside, a *mechoui*, a whole roast lamb or goat cooked over glowing coals in a pit in the ground. Next come a variety of savoury tagines, each one different, served with flat bread to mop up the tasty sauce.

The last tagine is always sweet, usually made of lamb, caramelized onions and honey. Just to make sure that no guest leaves with any space unfilled, the grand finale is a steaming mound of couscous, also eaten with the fingers.

Above: The clay tagine is central to Moroccan cooking.

Below: Mint tea is commonly drunk after every meal.

Mint tea, the classic refreshing Moroccan drink, is served afterwards to refresh the palate and aid digestion.

One of the most interesting ways to absorb the delights and diversity of a country's cuisine is to visit the markets. They are cool, spicy, colourful and noisy. Vegetables and fruit are piled high; leafy herbs are tied in bundles; simple white and yellow cheeses and slabs of butter are stacked in blocks; olive oil and local olives steep in deep vats; pickles, conserves and preserved lemons are displayed in huge jars or bowls; and there are nuts and dried fruit laid out.

The most remarkable of all the markets are the old, labyrinthine souks of Fez and Marrakech where, among the natural remedies of the apothecary, the drying lavender and rose buds, the most enticing characteristic is the aroma of exotic spices.

Classic Spice Blends

At the heart of Moroccan cooking are the spice mixes and flavourings that have been used for centuries. It is worth preparing some of the following basic recipes, as traditional ingredients such as hot harrisa paste and chermoula marinade are essential if you wish to create authentic Moroccan dishes. Most of these spicy flavourings can be purchased ready-made but they are also simple to make at home.

Preserved lemons are one of the most important ingredients used in Moroccan cuisine. With their tender rinds, jam-like consistency and intense flavour, they impart a distinctive taste to many dishes. The lemons can be preserved in salt, brine or oil, or they can be pickled, but salt and lemon juice is the most popular method.

Traditional spice mixes that play a key role in Moroccan food but originate from elsewhere are *tabil* from Tunisia and *zahtar* from the Middle East.

Ras el hanout

Of all the spice mixes of the Middle East and North Africa perhaps the most eloquent and refined is Morocco's *ras el hanout*. Known for its aphrodisiac qualities and for the poetry of the rose, it is both aromatic and spicy, warming every dish it graces. Beyond the spice bazaars of the Arab world, it would be difficult to make a genuine, pungent *ras el hanout* for the quantity and variety of spices required elude most stores: cardamoms from Sri Lanka; nutmeg and mace from Java; galangal from the Far East; guinea pepper, an aphrodisiac from the Ivory Coast; cinnamon from India and Sri Lanka; cloves from Zanzibar; ginger and curcuma from India; cyparacee, a strong-smelling stalk, from Sudan; orris root from high in the Atlas Mountains; white ginger from Japan; ash berries from Europe; monk's pepper from Morocco; belladonna berries; fennel flowers; lavender; black pepper; and rose buds.

Right: Spices in a typical market stall in the Souk, Marrakech. Left: You can buy ras el hanout from most North African and Arab Stores.

Chermoula

This hot, tasty marinade contributes its distinct flavour to many grilled (broiled) fish and vegetable dishes and to some tagines. There are many variations. Different herbs and spices may be used in varying proportions to produce wonderful results. Chermoula tends to be fairly hot and fiery so is particularly well suited to robustly flavoured meats and fish. This recipe makes enough for one dish.

2–3 garlic cloves, chopped
5–10ml/1–2 tsp ground cumin
pinch of saffron threads, soaked in a
    little water

60ml/4 tbsp olive oil
juice of 1 lemon
1 hot red chili, seeded and chopped
5ml/1 tsp salt
small bunch of fresh coriander
    (cilantro), finely chopped

Place all the ingredients except the coriander in a mortar and pound with a pestle. Alternatively, process briefly in a food processor. Add the fresh coriander and stir to combine.

Preserved Lemons

Known as *l'hamd mrakad* in Morocco, the intense flavour of preserved lemons lends a wonderful tang to many Moroccan dishes, from tagines to salads.

12 lemons
150ml/10 tbsp/¾ cup sea salt

Wash and dry the lemons, and set two aside. Cut a thin slice from the top and bottom of each of the remaining lemons. Stand a lemon on end and make one or two vertical cuts three-quarters of the way

through the fruit, making sure the two halves are still attached. Stuff the lemon with plenty of salt and repeat with the remaining fruit and salt. Pack the lemons into a jar so that they are squashed together.

Leave the lemons for 3–4 days to allow the skins to soften, then press them down again. Squeeze the juice from the reserved lemons and pour enough into the jar to cover the salted lemons completely. Store the lemons for at least a month before using. Simply rinse off the salt and use them according to the recipe.

Harissa

This hot sauce features strongly in North African cooking. Endlessly versatile, it can be used as a condiment, served with food according to individual tastes; it can be added to dishes to give them a fiery kick; or it can be served as a dip for warm bread, either on its own or blended with a little yogurt.

Traditionally, the ingredients are pounded to a paste using a pestle and mortar, but whizzing them in an electric blender is far simpler and quicker. This recipe makes a small amount for a dip, or enough for several dishes.

6–8 dried red chillies (preferably New Mexico variety), seeded
2 garlic cloves, crushed
2.5ml/½ tsp sea salt
5ml/1 tsp ground cumin
2.5ml/½ tsp ground coriander
120ml/4fl oz/1½ cup olive oil

Soak the chillies in warm water for about 40 minutes, until soft. Drain and squeeze out the excess water. Place them in a blender with the other ingredients and process the mixture to form a paste. Spoon the harissa into a small jar, cover with a layer of olive oil and seal tightly. Store in the refrigerator and use within 1 month.

Zahtar

This spice mixture is used to sprinkle over dips, fried vegetables and flat breads.

15ml/1 tbsp dried thyme
15ml/1 tbsp ground sumac
15ml/1 tbsp roasted sesame seeds
a sprinkling of coarse salt

Combine all the ingredients in a bowl. Store in an airtight jar.

Tabil

This Tunisian spice mixture gives a distinct flavour to tagines and vegetable dishes. It can be either a paste or a powder.

45ml/3 tbsp coriander seeds
15ml/1 tbsp caraway seeds
15ml/1 tbsp garlic powder or 2–3 garlic cloves
15ml/1 tbsp chilli powder or cayenne pepper or 1 dried red chilli, soaked

Place all the ingredients in a mortar and grind with a pestle to form a dry powder or paste.

Bottom: Zahtar (top) and Tabil (below) are two popular spice mixtures.

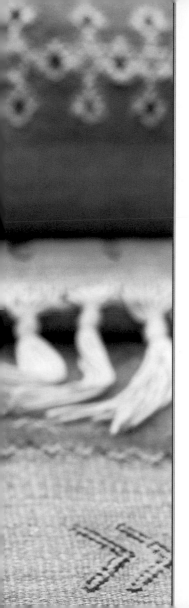

A Taste of Morocco

With a diverse culinary history that draws from the East, Africa, and the Mediterranean, Morocco is home to some of the most tantalizing food imaginable. The dishes please the eye as well as the palate, intoxicating you with their heady spices and sumptuous sauces. Simple cooking methods and traditional spice mixes make it easy to produce authentic Moroccan food at home. From a colourful mezze, rich in variety and exotic flavours, to a comforting tagine, infused with delicious aromas and sweetened with fruits, this collection of recipes offer an intriguing insight into the food and cooking of Morocco.

Left: Typical earthenware soup bowls ready to be filled with warming couscous or a steaming

Bissara Dip with Zahtar

Serves 4

350g/12oz/1¾ cups dried broad
   (fava) beans, soaked overnight
4 garlic cloves
10ml/2 tsp cumin seeds
60–75ml/4–5 tbsp olive oil
salt
zahtar, paprika or dried thyme to
   garnish

1 Drain the beans, remove their wrinkly skins and place them in a large pan with the garlic and cumin seeds. Add enough water to cover the beans and bring to the boil. Boil for 10 minutes, then reduce the heat, cover the pan and simmer gently for about 1 hour, or until the beans are tender.

2 When cooked, drain the beans and, while they are still warm, pound or process them with the olive oil until the mixture forms a smooth dip. Season to taste with salt and serve warm or at room temperature, sprinkled with zahtar, paprika or thyme. Alternatively, simply drizzle with a little olive oil.

This garlicky broad bean dip is enjoyed throughout Morocco. Sprinkled with the Middle-Eastern spice zahtar, paprika or dried thyme, it makes a tasty appetizer served with flat bread. It is particularly popular in the cafés of Fez and Marrakech, where Moroccans and tourists mingle over food.

Honey-spiced Artichoke Hearts

Serves 4

30–45ml/2–3 tbsp olive oil
2 garlic cloves, crushed
scant 5ml/1 tsp ground ginger
pinch of saffron threads
juice of ½ lemon
15–30ml/1–2 tbsp honey
peel of 1 preserved lemon, finely
  sliced
8 artichoke hearts, quartered
150ml/¼ pint/½ cup water
salt

When globe artichokes are in season, they grace every Moroccan table as a first course or salad. The hearts are often poached in salted water until tender, then chopped and tossed in olive oil with garlic, herbs and preserved lemon. For a more exciting appetizer, the artichokes are cooked in this glorious spiced honey dressing.

1 Heat the olive oil in a small heavy pan and stir in the garlic. Before the garlic begins to colour, stir in the ginger, saffron, lemon juice, honey and preserved lemon. Add the artichokes and toss them in the spices and honey. Pour in the water, add a little salt and heat until simmering.

2 Cover the pan and simmer for 10–15 minutes until the artichokes are tender, turning them occasionally. If the liquid has not reduced, take the lid off the pan and boil for about 2 minutes until reduced to a coating consistency. Serve warm or at room temperature.

PREPARING GLOBE ARTICHOKES

Remove the outer leaves and cut off the stems. Carefully separate the remaining leaves and use a teaspoon to scoop out the choke with all the hairy bits. Trim the hearts and immerse them in water mixed with a squeeze of lemon juice to prevent them from turning black.

Grilled Aubergine in Honey and Spices

1 Preheat the grill or broiler. Dip each aubergine slice in olive oil and cook in a pan under the grill. Turn the slices so that they are lightly browned on both sides.

2 In a wide frying pan, fry the garlic in a little olive oil for a few seconds, then stir in the ginger, cumin, harissa, honey and lemon juice. Add enough water to cover the base of the pan and to thin the mixture, then lay the aubergine slices in the pan. Cook the aubergines gently for about 10 minutes, or until they have absorbed all the sauce.

3 Add a little extra water, if necessary, season to taste with salt, and serve at room temperature, with chunks of fresh bread to mop up the delicious juices.

ALTERNATIVE FLAVOURINGS
Courgettes (zucchini) can also be cooked in this way. If you want to make a feature out of this sumptuous dish, serve it with other grilled or broiled vegetables and fruit, such as (bell) peppers, chillies, tomatoes, oranges, pineapple and mangoes.

Serves 4

2 aubergines (eggplant), peeled and
  thickly sliced
olive oil, for frying
2–3 garlic cloves, crushed
5cm/2in piece of fresh root ginger,
  peeled and grated
5ml/1 tsp ground cumin
5ml/1 tsp harissa
75ml/5 tbsp clear honey
juice of 1 lemon
salt

Hot, spicy, sweet and fruity are classic flavours of North African cooking and in this delicious Moroccan dish, their combination sends you on a thrilling journey. For a spread of tantalizing tastes, serve with artichoke heart and orange salad and the garlicky dip, bissara. Baby aubergines are very effective for this dish as you can slice them in half lengthways and hold them by their stalks.

Feta Cheese Cigars

Makes about 32

8 sheets of ouarka or filo pastry
sunflower oil, for deep-frying

For the feta cheese filling

450g/1lb feta cheese
4 eggs
bunch of fresh coriander (cilantro), finely chopped
bunch of flat leaf parsley, finely chopped
bunch of mint, finely chopped

1 To make the feta cheese filling, place the cheese in a bowl and mash with a fork, then beat in the eggs and chopped herbs.

2 Lay a sheet of ouarka or filo pastry on a work surface. Cut the sheet widthways into four strips. Spoon a little filling mixture on the first strip, at the end nearest to you.

3 Fold the corners of the pastry over the mixture to seal it, then roll up the pastry and filling away from you into a tight cigar. As you reach the end of the strip, brush the edges with a little water and continue to roll up the cigar to seal in the filling. Repeat, placing the finished cigars under a damp cloth.

4 Heat the sunflower oil for deep-frying to 180°C/350°F, or until a cube of day-old bread browns in 30–45 seconds. Add the cigars to the oil in batches and fry over a medium heat until golden brown. Drain on kitchen paper and serve warm.

Known as briouats *in Morocco, these little savoury pastries are filled with either minced or ground lamb or beef, spinach or cheese with herbs. Easy to make, they are always shaped into cigars or triangles and the fillings can be varied to suit individual tastes. The filling can be prepared ahead of time but the pastry should only be unwrapped when you are ready to make the pastries, otherwise it will dry out.*

Chunky Tomato Soup with Ras el Hanout and Noodles

1 In a deep, heavy pan, heat the oil and add the cloves, onions, squash, celery and carrots. Fry until they begin to colour, then stir in the tomatoes and sugar. Cook the tomatoes until the water reduces and they begin to pulp.

2 Stir in the tomato purée, ras el hanout, turmeric and chopped coriander. Pour in the stock and bring the liquid to the boil. Reduce the heat and simmer for 30–40 minutes until the vegetables are very tender and the liquid has reduced a little.

3 To make a puréed soup, leave the liquid to cool slightly before processing in a food processor or blender, then pour back into the pan and add the pasta.

4 Alternatively, to make a chunky soup, simply add the pasta to the unblended soup and cook for a further 8–10 minutes, or until the pasta is soft. Season the soup to taste and ladle it into bowls. Spoon a swirl of yogurt into each one, garnish with the extra coriander and serve with a freshly baked Moroccan loaf.

Serves 4

45–60ml/3–4 tbsp olive oil
3–4 cloves
2 onions, chopped
1 butternut squash, peeled, seeded and cut into small chunks
4 celery stalks, chopped
2 carrots, peeled and chopped
8 large, ripe tomatoes, skinned and roughly chopped
5–10ml/1–2 tsp sugar
15ml/1 tbsp tomato purée (paste)
5–10ml/1–2 tsp ras el hanout
2.5ml/½ tsp ground turmeric
a big bunch of fresh coriander (cilantro), chopped (reserve a few sprigs for garnish)
1.8 litres/3 pints/7½ cups vegetable stock
a handful dried egg noodles or capellini, broken into pieces
salt and ground black pepper
60–75ml/4–5 tbsp creamy yogurt, to serve

This full-flavoured chorba is the daily soup in many Moroccan households. The ras el hanout gives it a lovely, warming kick. You can purée the soup, if you prefer, but I like it just as it is, finished off with a swirl of yogurt and finely chopped coriander. Garlic lovers may like to add a crushed garlic clove and a little salt to the yogurt. Serve with chunks of fresh bread.

Sesame-coated Majoun

Makes about 20
500g/1¼lb blanched almonds
250g/9oz/1½ cups walnuts
500g/1¼lb raisins
130g/4½oz/generous ½ cup butter
250g/9oz/generous 1 cup clear
    honey
7.5ml/1½ tsp ras el hanout
7.5ml/1½ tsp ground ginger
60–75g/4–5oz sesame seeds

You will find these sweet, spicy fruit and nut balls on every street corner in Morocco. The quantity of spices varies from cook to cook, and the secret to their delicious flavour is often in the amount of hashish used. For these are the infamous hashish balls, popular as a narcotic or as an aphrodisiac; however in this version the hashish is omitted (with some detriment to flavour!).

1 Finely chop the almonds, walnuts and raisins in a food processor or blender until they form a coarse, slightly sticky mixture. Alternatively, pound these ingredients together in batches in a large mortar using a pestle until the correct consistency is reached – you will need to do this in batches.

2 Melt the butter in a large heavy pan and stir in the honey, ras el hanout and ginger. Add the nuts and raisins and stir over a gentle heat for a few seconds until the mixture is thoroughly combined, firm and sticky. Cool a little, then shape into about 20 balls. Roll the balls in sesame seeds to coat completely.

Pan-fried Baby Squid with Spices

Serves 4

8 baby squid, prepared, with
   tentacles
5ml/1 tsp ground turmeric
15ml/1 tbsp smen or olive oil
2 garlic cloves, finely chopped
15g/½ oz fresh root ginger, peeled
   and finely chopped
5–10ml/1–2 tsp honey
juice of 1 lemon
10ml/2 tsp harissa
salt
small bunch of fresh coriander
   (cilantro), roughly chopped, to
   serve

1 Pat dry the squid bodies, inside and out, and dry the tentacles. Sprinkle the squid and tentacles with the ground turmeric.

2 Heat the smen or olive oil in a large heavy frying pan and stir in the garlic and ginger. Just as the ginger and garlic begin to colour, add the squid and tentacles and fry quickly on both sides over a high heat. (Don't overcook the squid, otherwise it will become rubbery.)

3 Add the honey, lemon juice and harissa and stir to form a thick, spicy, caramelized sauce. Season with salt, sprinkle with the chopped coriander and serve immediately.

You have to work quickly to prepare this dish, then serve it immediately, so that the squid is just cooked and tender. The flavours of turmeric, ginger and harissa are fabulous with the sweet honey and zesty lemon juice.

Bus-station Kefta with Egg and Tomato

1 In a bowl, knead the minced lamb with the onion, breadcrumbs, 1 egg, cinnamon, parsley and salt and pepper until well mixed. Lift the mixture in your hand and slap it down into the bowl several times. Take a small amount of mixture and shape it into a small ball about the size of a walnut. Repeat with the remaining mixture to make about 12 balls.

2 Heat the olive oil with the butter in a large heavy frying pan. Fry the meatballs until nicely browned, turning them occasionally so they cook evenly. Stir in the tomatoes, sugar, ras el hanout and most of the coriander. Bring to the boil, cook for a few minutes to reduce the liquid, and roll the balls in the sauce. Season to taste with salt and pepper.

3 Make room for the remaining 4 eggs in the pan and crack them into spaces between the meatballs. Cover the pan, reduce the heat and cook for about 3 minutes or until the eggs are just set. Sprinkle with the remaining coriander and serve in the pan, with chunks of bread to use as scoops.

Serves 4

225g/8oz finely minced (ground) lamb
1 onion, finely chopped
50g/2oz fresh breadcrumbs
5 eggs
5ml/1 tsp ground cinnamon
small bunch of flat leaf parsley, finely chopped
30ml/2 tbsp olive oil
a little butter
400g/14oz can chopped tomatoes
10ml/2 tsp sugar
5ml/1 tsp ras el hanout
small bunch of fresh coriander (cilantro), roughly chopped
salt and ground black pepper
crusty bread, to serve

Egg and tomato dishes are very popular in bus and train stations and ports around the Middle East and North Africa. Travellers waiting for connecting transport services tuck into dishes like this to sustain themselves during long journeys. The dish is always eaten out of the pan in which it is cooked. It would make a great informal brunch or supper dish.

Casablancan Couscous with Roasted Summer Vegetables

Serves 6

3 red onions, peeled and quartered
2–3 courgettes (zucchini), halved
    lengthways and cut across into
    2–3 pieces
2–3 red, green or yellow (bell)
    peppers, seeded and quartered
2 aubergines (eggplant), cut into 6–8
    long segments
2–3 leeks, trimmed and cut into long
    strips
2–3 sweet potatoes, peeled, halved
    lengthways and cut into long strips
4–6 tomatoes, quartered
6 garlic cloves, crushed
25g/1oz fresh root ginger, sliced
a few fresh rosemary sprigs
about 150ml/¼ pint/⅔ cup olive oil
10ml/2 tsp sugar or clear honey
salt and ground black pepper
natural (plain) yogurt or harissa and
    bread, to serve

For the couscous

500g/1¼ lb/3 cups medium
    couscous
5ml/1 tsp salt
600ml/1 pint/2½ cups warm water
45ml/3 tbsp sunflower oil
about 25g/1oz/2 tbsp butter, diced

1 Preheat the oven to 200°C/400°F/Gas 6. Arrange all the vegetables in a roasting pan. Tuck the garlic, ginger and rosemary around the vegetables. Pour lots of olive oil over the vegetables, sprinkle with the sugar or honey, salt and pepper, and roast for about 1½ hours until they are extremely tender and slightly caramelized. The cooking time will depend on the size of the vegetable pieces. Turn them in the oil occasionally.

2 When the vegetables are nearly ready, put the couscous in a bowl. Stir the salt into the water, then pour it over the couscous, stirring to make sure it is absorbed evenly. Leave to stand for 10 minutes to plump up then, using your fingers, rub the sunflower oil into the grains to air them and break up any lumps. Tip the couscous into an ovenproof dish, arrange the butter over the top, cover with foil and heat in the oven for about 20 minutes.

3 To serve, use your fingers to work the melted butter into the grains of couscous and fluff it up, then pile it on a large dish and shape into a mound with a little pit at the top. Spoon some vegetables into the pit and arrange the rest around the dish. Pour the oil from the pan over the couscous or serve separately. Serve immediately with yogurt, or harissa if you prefer, and bread for mopping up the juices.

This dish is based on the classic couscous recipe for a stew containing seven vegetables. The number seven is believed to bring good luck. I like to serve this dish with a dollop of thick and creamy yogurt but, if you wish, you can also serve it with a spoonful of fiery harissa as a condiment.

Spicy Couscous with Aromatic Shellfish Broth

1 Preheat the oven to 180°C/350°F/Gas 4. Place the medium couscous in a large bowl. Stir the salt into the water, then pour over the couscous, stirring. Set aside for 10 minutes.

2 Stir the sunflower oil into the harissa to make a paste, then, using your fingers, rub it into the couscous and break up any lumps. Tip into an ovenproof dish, arrange the butter over, cover with foil and heat in the oven for about 20 minutes.

3 Meanwhile, put the mussels and prawns in a pan, add the lemon juice and 50ml/2fl oz/¼ cup water, cover and cook for 3–4 minutes, shaking the pan, until the mussels have opened. Drain the shellfish, reserving the liquor, and shell about two-thirds of the mussels and prawns. Discard any closed mussels.

4 Heat the butter in a large pan. Cook the shallots for 5 minutes, or until softened. Add the spices and fry for 1 minute. Off the heat, stir in the flour, the fish stock and shellfish cooking liquor. Bring to the boil, stirring. Add the cream and simmer, stirring occasionally, for about 10 minutes. Season with salt and pepper, add the shellfish and most of the fresh coriander. Heat through, then sprinkle with the remaining coriander.

5 Fluff up the couscous with a fork or your fingers, working in the melted butter. To serve, pass round the cooked couscous and ladle the broth over the top.

ROASTING SPICES
Toss the spices in a heavy pan over a high heat until they begin to change colour and give off a nutty aroma, then immediately tip them into a bowl.

Some couscous dishes include a soup-like stew, which is ladled over the cooked couscous and mopped up with lots of bread.

Serves 4–6

500g/1¼ lb/3 cups medium couscous
5ml/1 tsp salt
600ml/1 pint/2½ cups warm water
45ml/3 tbsp sunflower oil
5–10ml/1–2 tsp harissa
25g/1oz/2 tbsp butter, diced

For the shellfish broth

500g/1¼ lb mussels in their shells, scrubbed with beards removed
500g/1¼ lb uncooked prawns (shrimp) in their shells
juice of 1 lemon
50g/2oz/2 tbsp butter
2 shallots, finely chopped
5ml/1 tsp coriander seeds, roasted and ground
5ml/1 tsp cumin seeds, roasted and ground
2.5ml/½ tsp ground turmeric
2.5ml/½ tsp cayenne pepper
5–10ml/1–2 tsp plain (all-purpose) flour
600ml/1 pint/2½ cups fish stock
120ml/4fl oz/½ cup double (heavy) cream
salt and ground black pepper
small bunch of fresh coriander (cilantro), finely chopped, to serve

Tagine of Lamb with Crunchy Country Salad

Serves 6

1kg/2¼lb boneless shoulder of lamb,
    trimmed and cubed
30–45ml/2–3 tbsp vegetable oil
25g/1oz fresh root ginger, peeled and
    chopped
pinch of saffron threads
10ml/2 tsp ground cinnamon
1 onion, finely chopped
2–3 garlic cloves, chopped
350g/12oz/1½ cups pitted prunes,
    soaked for 1 hour
30ml/2 tbsp clear honey
salt and ground black pepper

For the salad

2 onions, chopped
1 red (bell) pepper, seeded and
    chopped
1 green (bell) pepper, seeded and
    chopped
2–3 celery sticks, chopped
2–3 green chillies, seeded and
    chopped
2 garlic cloves, chopped
30ml/2 tbsp olive oil
juice of ½ lemon
small bunch of parsley, chopped
a little mint, chopped

1 Put the meat in a flameproof casserole or heavy pan. Add the oil, ginger, saffron, cinnamon, onion, garlic and seasoning, then pour in enough water to cover. Heat until just simmering, cover with a lid and simmer gently for about 2 hours, topping up the water if necessary, until the meat is very tender.

2 Drain the prunes and add them to the tagine. Stir in the honey and simmer for a further 30 minutes, or until the sauce has reduced.

3 To make the salad, mix the onions, peppers, celery, chillies and garlic in a bowl. Pour the olive oil and lemon juice over the vegetables and toss to coat. Season with salt and add the parsley and mint. Serve the hot lamb tagine with the chilli-laced salad.

Morocco's hearty tagines are well known for their succulent meat cooked in a combination of honey and warm spices. This delicious recipe is for one of the most traditional and popular tagines, which is best served with a crunchy salad, spiked with chilli to balance the sweetness of the main dish. Offer lots of fresh bread for mopping up the thick, syrupy sauce.

Tagine of Artichoke Hearts, Potatoes, Peas and Saffron

Serves 4–6

6 fresh artichoke hearts
juice of 1 lemon
30–45ml/2–3 tbsp olive oil
1 onion, chopped
675g/1½ lb potatoes, peeled and quartered
small bunch of flat leaf parsley, chopped
small bunch of coriander (cilantro), chopped
small bunch of mint, chopped
pinch of saffron threads
5ml/1 tsp ground turmeric
about 350ml/12fl oz/1½ cups vegetable stock
finely chopped rind of ½ preserved lemon
250g/9oz/2¼ cups shelled peas
salt and ground black pepper
couscous or bread, to serve

1 Poach the artichoke hearts very gently in plenty of simmering water with half the lemon juice, for 10–15 minutes until tender. Drain and refresh under cold running water, then drain again.

2 Heat the olive oil in a tagine or heavy pan. Add the chopped onion and cook gently for about 15 minutes, or until softened but not browned. Add the potatoes, most of the parsley, the coriander, mint, the remaining lemon juice, and the saffron and turmeric to the pan. Pour in the vegetable stock, bring to the boil, then reduce the heat. Cover the pan and cook for about 15 minutes, or until the potatoes are almost tender.

3 Stir the preserved lemon rind, artichoke hearts and peas into the stew, and cook, uncovered, for a further 10 minutes. Season to taste, sprinkle with the remaining parsley, and serve with couscous or fresh bread.

PREPARING ARTICHOKES
Once cut, the flesh of artichokes will blacken. To prevent this from happening, put the artichokes into acidulated water – you can use lemon juice or white wine vinegar.

When artichokes are in season, this succulent tagine is a favourite country dish made using other produce from the garden. Fresh coriander, parsley and mint combine to complement the summery flavours of the vegetables while turmeric contributes its earthy warmth. Prepare the artichokes yourself by removing the outer leaves, cutting off the stems, and scooping out the choke and hairy bits with a teaspoon, or buy frozen prepared hearts.

Tagine of Monkfish, Potatoes, Cherry Tomatoes and Olives

1 Use a mortar and pestle to make the chermoula: pound the garlic with the salt to a smooth paste. Add the cumin, paprika, lemon juice and coriander, and gradually mix in the olive oil to emulsify the mixture slightly. Reserve a little chermoula for cooking, then rub the rest of the paste over the chunks of monkfish. Cover and leave to marinate for about 1 hour.

2 Par-boil the potatoes for about 10 minutes until slightly softened. Drain, refresh under cold water and drain again, then cut them in half lengthways. Heat the olive oil in a heavy pan and stir in the garlic. When the garlic begins to colour, add the tomatoes and cook until just softened. Add the peppers and the remaining chermoula, and season with salt and pepper.

3 Spread the potatoes over the base of a tagine, shallow pan or deep, ridged frying pan. Spoon three-quarters of the tomato and pepper mixture over and place the marinated fish chunks on top, with their marinade.

4 Spoon the rest of the tomato and pepper mixture on top of the fish and add the olives. Drizzle a little extra olive oil over the dish and pour in the water. Heat until simmering, cover the tagine or pan with a lid and steam over a medium heat for about 15 minutes, or until the fish is cooked through.

The fish for this tagine is marinated in chermoula, which gives it that unmistakable Moroccan flavour. It is a delightful dish at any time of year but it is especially good made with full-flavoured, new season potatoes and little sun-ripened cherry tomatoes.

Serves 4
900g/2lb monkfish tail, cut into chunks
15–20 small new potatoes, scrubbed, scraped or peeled
45–60ml/3–4 tbsp olive oil
4–5 garlic cloves, thinly sliced
15–20 cherry tomatoes
2 green (bell) peppers, grilled (broiled) until black, skinned, seeded and cut into strips
large handful of kalamata or fleshy black olives
100ml/3½fl oz/scant ½ cup water
salt and ground black pepper

For the chermoula
2 garlic cloves
5ml/1 tsp coarse salt
10ml/2 tsp ground cumin
5ml/1 tsp paprika
juice of 1 lemon
small bunch of fresh coriander (cilantro), roughly chopped
15ml/1 tbsp olive oil

Tagine of Spiced Kefta with Lemon and Spices

1 To make the kefta, pound the minced lamb in a bowl by using your hand to lift it up and slap it back down into the bowl. Knead in half the grated onions, the parsley, cinnamon, cumin and cayenne pepper. Season with salt and pepper, and continue pounding the mixture by hand for a few minutes. Break off pieces of the mixture and shape them into walnut-size balls.

2 In a heavy lidded frying pan, melt the butter and add the remaining onion with the ginger, chilli and saffron. Stirring frequently, cook just until the onion begins to colour, then stir in the coriander and lemon juice. Pour in the water, season with salt and bring to the boil. Drop in the kefta, reduce the heat and cover the pan. Poach the kefta gently, turning them occasionally, for about 20 minutes.

3 Remove the lid, tuck the lemon quarters around the kefta and cook, uncovered, for a further 10 minutes to reduce the liquid slightly. Serve hot, straight from the pan with lots of crusty fresh bread to mop up the delicious juices.

Serves 4

450g/1lb finely minced (ground) lamb
3 large onions, grated
small bunch of flat leaf parsley, chopped
5–10ml/1–2 tsp ground cinnamon
5ml/1 tsp ground cumin
pinch of cayenne pepper
40g/1½oz/3 tbsp butter
25g/1oz fresh root ginger, peeled and finely chopped
1 hot chilli, seeded and finely chopped
pinch of saffron threads
small bunch of fresh coriander (cilantro), finely chopped
juice of 1 lemon
300ml/½ pint/1¼ cups water
1 lemon, quartered
salt and ground black pepper

The kefta, or meatballs, are poached gently with lemon and spices to make a dish that is quite light and ideal for lunch. Serve it with a salad or plain couscous. In Morocco today, this dish has no boundaries. It can be found in the tiniest rural villages, in street stalls in the towns and cities, or in the finest restaurants of Casablanca, Fez and Marrakech.

Summer Vegetable Kebabs with Harissa and Yogurt Dip

Serves 4

2 aubergines (eggplant), part peeled and cut into chunks
2 courgettes (zucchini), cut into chunks
2–3 red or green (bell) peppers, seeded and cut into chunks
12–16 cherry tomatoes
4 small red onions, quartered
60ml/4 tbsp olive oil
juice of ½ lemon
1 garlic clove, crushed
5ml/1 tsp ground coriander
5ml/1 tsp ground cinnamon
10ml/2 tsp clear honey
5ml/1 tsp salt

For the harissa and yogurt dip

450g/1lb/2 cups Greek (US strained plain) yogurt
30–60ml/2–4 tbsp harissa
small bunch of fresh coriander (cilantro), finely chopped
small bunch of mint, finely chopped
salt and ground black pepper

1 Preheat the grill or broiler on the hottest setting. Put all the vegetables in a bowl. Mix the olive oil, lemon juice, garlic, ground coriander, cinnamon, honey and salt and pour the mixture over the vegetables. Using your hands, turn the vegetables gently in the marinade, then thread them on to metal skewers.

2 Cook the kebabs under the grill, turning them occasionally until the vegetables are nicely browned all over.

3 To make the dip, put the yogurt in a bowl and beat in the harissa, making it as fiery as you like by adding more harissa. Add most of the coriander and mint, reserving a little to garnish, and season well with salt and pepper.

4 While they are still hot, slide the vegetables off the skewers and dip them into the yogurt dip before eating. Garnish with the reserved herbs.

PREPARING THE VEGETABLES
Make sure you cut the aubergines, courgettes and peppers into fairly even-size chunks, so they will all cook at the same rate.

This simple and tasty vegetarian dish is delicious served with couscous and a fresh, crispy green salad. It also makes an excellent side dish to accompany meat-based main courses. In Morocco today, vegetable and fish kebabs are becoming increasingly popular in fashionable restaurants and households, where there is a tendency to move away from the traditional meat-based meals.

Spiced Sardines with Grapefruit and Fennel Salad

Serves 4–6

12 fresh sardines, cleaned and gutted
coarse salt
1 onion, grated
60–90ml/4–6 tbsp olive oil
5ml/1 tsp ground cinnamon
10ml/2 tsp cumin seeds, roasted and ground
10ml/2 tsp coriander seeds, roasted and ground
5ml/1 tsp paprika
5ml/1 tsp ground black pepper
small bunch of fresh coriander (cilantro), chopped
2 lemons, cut into wedges, to serve

For the salad

2 ruby grapefruits
5ml/1 tsp sea salt
1 fennel bulb
2–3 spring onions (scallions), finely sliced
2.5ml/½ tsp ground roasted cumin
30–45ml/2–3 tbsp olive oil
handful of black olives

1 Rinse the sardines and pat them dry on kitchen paper, then rub inside and out with a little coarse salt. In a bowl, mix the grated onion with the olive oil, cinnamon, ground roasted cumin and coriander, paprika and black pepper. Make several slashes into the flesh of the sardines and smear the onion and spice mixture all over the fish, inside and out and into the gashes. Leave the sardines to stand for about 1 hour to allow the flavours of the spices to penetrate the flesh.

2 Meanwhile, prepare the salad. Peel the grapefruits with a knife, removing all the pith and peel in neat strips down the outside of the fruit. Cut between the membranes to remove the segments of fruit intact. Cut each grapefruit segment in half, place in a bowl and sprinkle with salt. Trim the fennel, cut it in half lengthways and slice finely. Add the fennel to the grapefruit with the spring onions, cumin and olive oil. Toss lightly, then garnish with the olives.

3 Preheat the grill or broiler or barbecue. Cook the sardines for 3–4 minutes on each side, basting with any leftover marinade. Sprinkle with fresh coriander and serve immediately, with lemon wedges for squeezing over and the refreshing grapefruit and fennel salad.

Sardines spiced with cumin and coriander are popular in the coastal regions of Morocco, both in restaurants and as street food. In Tangier, I ate them from a street stall, where they were cleaned and smeared with a spicy paste, dredged with flour and deep-fried, then sandwiched between two bits of bread with a handful of fresh coriander.

Fiery Chicken Wings with Blood Oranges

1 Put the harissa in a small bowl with the olive oil and mix to form a loose paste. Add a little salt and stir to combine.

2 Brush this mixture over the chicken wings so that they are well coated. Cook the wings on a hot barbecue or under a hot grill or broiler, for 5 minutes on each side.

3 Once the wings begin to cook, dip the orange quarters lightly in icing sugar and grill them for a few minutes, until they are slightly burnt but not black and charred.

4 Serve the chicken wings immediately with the oranges, sprinkled with a little chopped fresh coriander.

Serves 4

60ml/4 tbsp fiery harissa
30ml/2 tbsp olive oil
16–20 chicken wings
4 blood oranges, quartered
icing (confectioners') sugar
small bunch of fresh coriander
   (cilantro), chopped
salt

This is a great recipe for the barbecue – it is quick and easy, and best eaten with the fingers. The juicy oranges are there to suck after experiencing an explosion of fiery spices on the tongue. The oranges can be cooked separately or threaded alternately with the chicken wings on skewers. Cherry tomatoes can be used as well, as it is the burst of juice that makes this dish so delicious.

Spicy Beef Kebabs with Hot Chickpea Purée

Serves 6

500g/1¼ lb finely minced (ground)
  beef
1 onion, grated
10ml/2 tsp ground cumin
10ml/2 tsp ground coriander
10ml/2 tsp paprika
4ml/¾ tsp cayenne pepper
5ml/1 tsp salt
small bunch of flat leaf parsley, finely
  chopped
small bunch of fresh coriander
  (cilantro), finely chopped

For the chickpea purée

225g/8oz/1¼ cups dried chickpeas,
  soaked overnight, drained and
  cooked
50ml/2fl oz/¼ cup olive oil
juice of 1 lemon
2 garlic cloves, crushed
5ml/1 tsp cumin seeds
30ml/2 tbsp light tahini
60ml/4 tbsp thick Greek (US strained
  plain) yogurt
40g/1½ oz/3 tbsp butter, melted
salt and ground black pepper

1 Mix the minced beef with the onion, cumin, ground coriander, paprika, cayenne, salt, parsley and chopped fresh coriander. Knead the mixture well, then pound it until smooth in a mortar with a pestle or in a food processor. Place in a dish, cover and leave to stand for 1 hour.

2 Meanwhile, make the chickpea purée. Preheat the oven to 200°C/400°F/Gas 6. In a food processor, process the chickpeas with the olive oil, lemon juice, garlic, cumin seeds, tahini and yogurt. Season, tip into an ovenproof dish, cover with foil and heat through for 20 minutes.

3 Divide the meat mixture into six portions and mould each on to a metal skewer, so that the meat resembles a fat sausage. Heat the grill or broiler on the hottest setting and cook the kebabs for 4–5 minutes on each side.

4 Melt the butter and pour it over the hot chickpea purée. Serve the kebabs with the hot chickpea purée.

Try this dish for a summer barbecue. Make the kebabs as fiery as you like by adding more cayenne pepper. The smooth, soothing chickpea purée adds a sumptuous touch. You need metal skewers with wide blades for these kebabs to hold the pounded meat in place so that it resembles a sheath on a sword when serving. The whole sheath can be pushed off the skewer. Serve with a green salad and bread.

Beetroot Salad with Oranges

Serves 4–6

675g/1½ lb beetroot (beet), steamed
or boiled, then peeled
1 orange, peeled and sliced
30ml/2 tbsp orange flower water
15ml/1 tbsp sugar
5ml/1 tsp ground cinnamon
salt and ground black pepper

1 Quarter the cooked beetroot, then slice the quarters. Arrange the beetroot on a plate with the orange slices or toss them together in a bowl. Gently heat the orange flower water with the sugar, stir in the cinnamon and season to taste. Pour the sweet mixture over the beetroot and orange salad and chill for at least 1 hour before serving.

COOKING BEETROOT

To cook raw beetroot always leave the skin on and trim off only the tops of the leaf stalks. Cook in boiling water or steam over rapidly boiling water for 1–2 hours, depending on size. Small beetroot are tender in about 1 hour, medium roots take 1–1½ hours, and larger roots can take up to 2 hours.

This salad can be made with bought vacuum-pack cooked beetroot (beet) or freshly steamed or boiled vegetables. The mix of sweet beetroot, zesty orange and warm cinnamon is both unusual and delicious, and this dish provides a burst of colour in a summer buffet spread.

Sautéed Herb Salad

Serves 4

large bunch of flat leaf parsley
large bunch of mint
large bunch of fresh coriander
(cilantro)
bunch of rocket (arugula)
large bunch of spinach leaves (about
115g/4oz)
60–75ml/4–5 tbsp olive oil
2 garlic cloves, finely chopped
1 green or red chilli, seeded and
finely chopped
½ preserved lemon, finely chopped
salt and ground black pepper
45–60ml/3–4 tbsp Greek (US
strained plain) yogurt, to serve

*Firm-leafed fresh herbs,
tossed in a little olive oil and
seasoned with salt, are
fabulous to serve as a salad
in a mezze spread or go
wonderfully with spicy
kebabs or tagines. Lightly
sautéed with garlic and
served warm with yogurt,
this dish is delightful even
on its own.*

1 Roughly chop the herbs, rocket and spinach. Heat the olive oil in a wide, heavy pan. Stir in the garlic and chilli, and fry until they begin to colour. Toss in the herbs, rocket and spinach and cook gently, until they begin to soften and wilt. Add the preserved lemon and season to taste. Serve the salad warm with a dollop of yogurt.

MAKING GARLIC-FLAVOURED YOGURT

Crush a clove of garlic and stir it into the yogurt with salt and ground pepper to taste.

Broad Bean Salad and Carrot Salad

Serves 4
For the broad bean salad

2kg/4½lb broad (fava) beans in the pod
60–75ml/4–5 tbsp olive oil
juice of ½ lemon
2 garlic cloves, chopped
5ml/1 tsp ground cumin
10ml/2 tsp paprika
small bunch of fresh coriander (cilantro), finely chopped
1 preserved lemon, chopped
handful of black olives, to garnish
salt and ground black pepper

Serves 4
For the carrot salad

450g/1lb carrots, cut into sticks
30–45ml/2–3 tbsp olive oil
juice of 1 lemon
2–3 garlic cloves, crushed
10ml/2 tsp sugar
5–10ml/1–2 tsp cumin seeds, roasted
5ml/1 tsp ground cinnamon
5ml/1 tsp paprika
small bunch of fresh coriander (cilantro), finely chopped
small bunch of mint, finely chopped
salt and ground black pepper

1 To make the broad bean salad, bring a large pan of salted water to the boil. Meanwhile, pod the beans. Put the beans in the pan and boil for about 2 minutes, then drain and refresh the beans under cold running water. Drain well. Slip off and discard the thick outer skin to reveal the smooth, bright green beans underneath.

2 Put the beans in a heavy pan and add the olive oil, lemon juice, garlic, cumin and paprika. Cook the beans gently over a low heat for 10 minutes, then season to taste and leave to cool in the pan.

3 Tip the beans into a serving bowl, scraping all the juices from the pan. Toss in the fresh coriander and preserved lemon and garnish with the black olives.

4 To make the carrot salad, steam the carrots over boiling water for 15 minutes, or until tender. While they are still warm, toss the carrots in a serving bowl with the olive oil, lemon juice, garlic and sugar. Season to taste, then add the cumin seeds, cinnamon and paprika. Finally, toss in the fresh coriander and mint, and serve warm or at room temperature.

ROASTING CUMIN SEEDS
Stir the cumin seeds in a heavy pan over a low heat until they change colour slightly and emit a warm, nutty aroma.

Throughout the Middle East, North Africa and the Mediterranean region, broad beans are a popular addition to salads and rice dishes but, in Morocco, the addition of preserved lemons gives this salad a distinct and appealing taste. The refreshing carrot salad is often served as an appetizer but, if you prefer, serve it warm for supper with tangy, garlic-flavoured yogurt.

Pomegranate Yogurt with Grapefruit Salad

Serves 3–4

300ml/½ pint/1¼ cups Greek
    (US strained plain) yogurt
2–3 ripe pomegranates
small bunch of mint, finely chopped
honey or sugar, to taste (optional)

For the grapefruit salad

2 red grapefruit
2 pink grapefruit
1 white grapefruit
15–30ml/1–2 tbsp orange flower
    water
handful of pomegranate seeds and
    mint leaves, to decorate

In this Moroccan dessert pomegranate seeds add texture, flavour and colour to a simple dish. You can eat this yogurt for breakfast or during the day for a healthy snack but it makes a fabulous dessert served with a delicately scented citrus fruit salad.

1 Put the yogurt in a bowl and beat well. Cut open the pomegranates and scoop out the seeds, removing all the bitter pith. Fold the pomegranate seeds and chopped mint into the yogurt. Sweeten with a little honey or sugar, if using, then chill until ready to serve.

2 Peel the red, pink and white grapefruits, cutting off all the pith. Cut between the membranes to remove the segments, holding the fruit over a bowl to catch the juices.

3 Discard the membranes and mix the fruit segments with the reserved juices. Sprinkle with the orange flower water. Stir gently then decorate with a few pomegranate seeds.

4 Add a dollop of the yogurt on top of the grapefruit salad and decorate with a few pomegranate seeds and mint leaves.

Poached Pears in Scented Honey Syrup

Serves 4

45ml/3 tbsp clear honey
juice of 1 lemon
250ml/8fl oz/1 cup water
pinch of saffron threads
1 cinnamon stick
2–3 dried lavender heads
4 firm pears

1 Heat the honey and lemon juice in a heavy pan that will hold the pears snugly. Stir over a gentle heat until the honey has dissolved. Add the water, saffron threads, cinnamon stick and flowers from 1–2 lavender heads. Bring the mixture to the boil, then reduce the heat and simmer for 5 minutes.

2 Peel the pears, leaving the stalks attached. Add the pears to the pan and simmer for 20 minutes, turning and basting at regular intervals, until they are tender. Leave the pears to cool in the syrup and serve at room temperature, decorated with a few lavender flowers.

Fruit has been poached in honey since ancient times. The Romans did it, as did the Persians, Arabs, Moors and Ottomans. The Moroccans continue the tradition today, adding a little orange rind or aniseed, or even lavender to give a subtle flavouring. Delicate and pretty to look at, these scented pears provide an exquisite finishing touch to a Moroccan meal.

Burnt Mulhalbia with Rose-petal Jam

1 In a bowl, combine the rice flour with a little of the milk to form a thin paste. Pour the remaining milk into a pan. Add the sugar and bring it to the boil, stirring all the time.

2 Reduce the heat and stir a spoonful or two of the hot milk into the rice flour paste, then pour the paste into the pan. Bring the mixture to the boil, stirring continuously. Add the orange flower water, then reduce the heat and simmer gently for 20–25 minutes, stirring occasionally, until the mixture becomes quite thick. Pour the mixture into flameproof serving bowls and leave to cool, allowing a skin to form on top.

3 Preheat the grill (broiler) on the hottest setting. Sprinkle each dessert liberally with caster sugar and place under the grill until the sugar melts and browns, taking care to remove the dessert before the sugar burns. Cool and then chill. Serve topped with a little warmed rose petal jam.

Serves 4–6

50g/2oz/⅓ cup rice flour
900ml/1½ pints/3¾ cups milk
115g/4oz/⅔ cup caster (superfine)
    sugar, plus 30–45ml/2–3 tbsp, for
    sprinkling
15ml/1 tbsp orange flower water
30–45ml/2–3 tbsp rose petal jam, to
    serve

This classic milk pudding, which features throughout the Middle East and North Africa, is flavoured with orange flower water but you can use rose water or vanilla. The Moroccan version is usually decorated with ground almonds and cinnamon, but, for a change, here the top is caramelized and finished with a little rose petal jam. You can make rose petal jam with the scented petals from your garden, but the jam is also available in most Middle Eastern stores.

Yogurt Cake with Pistachio Nuts, Crème Fraîche and Passion Fruit

Serves 4–6

3 eggs, separated

75g/3oz/scant ½ cup caster (superfine) sugar

seeds from 2 vanilla pods (beans)

300ml/½ pint/1¼ cups Greek (US strained plain) yogurt

grated rind and juice of 1 lemon

scant 15ml/1 tbsp plain (all-purpose) flour

handful of pistachio nuts, roughly chopped

60–90ml/4–6 tbsp crème fraîche and 4–6 fresh passion fruit or 50g/2oz/½ cup summer berries, to serve

1 Preheat the oven to 180°C/350°F/Gas 4. Line a 25cm/10in square, heatproof dish with greaseproof (waxed) paper and grease well.

2 Beat the egg yolks with two-thirds of the sugar, until pale and fluffy. Beat in the vanilla seeds and stir in the yogurt, lemon rind and juice, and the flour.

3 In a separate bowl, whisk the egg whites until stiff, then gradually whisk in the rest of the sugar to form soft peaks. Fold the whisked whites into the yogurt mixture. Turn the mixture into the prepared dish.

4 Place the dish in a roasting pan and pour in cold water to come about halfway up the outside of the dish. Bake for about 20 minutes until the mixture is risen and just set. Sprinkle the pistachio nuts over the cake and cook for a further 20 minutes, until browned on top.

5 Serve the cake warm or chilled with crème fraîche and a spoonful of passion fruit drizzled over the top. Alternatively, sprinkle with a few summer berries such as redcurrants, blackcurrants and blueberries.

Some yogurt cakes are dry and served with tea, others are bathed in lemon syrup and served at room temperature, and then there is this type, which is delicious warm or chilled with a dollop of crème fraîche or yogurt and a spoonful of fresh passion fruit. In Morocco this type of moist cake isn't necessarily reserved for dessert; it can be enjoyed at any time of day.

Serves 8–10

115g/4oz/1 cup blanched almonds
115g/4oz/½ cup butter, softened,
   plus 20g/¾oz for cooking nuts
300g/11oz/2¾ cups ground almonds
50g/2oz/½ cup icing (confectioners')
   sugar
115g/4oz/⅔ cup caster (superfine)
   sugar
5–10ml/1–2 tsp ground cinnamon
15ml/1 tbsp orange flower water
3–4 sheets filo pastry
1 egg yolk

For the topping

icing (confectioners') sugar
ground cinnamon

M'hanncha

1 Fry the blanched almonds in a little butter until golden brown, then pound them using a pestle and mortar until they resemble coarse breadcrumbs. Place the nuts in a bowl and add the ground almonds, icing sugar, caster sugar, remaining butter, cinnamon and orange flower water. Use your hands to form the mixture into a smooth paste. Cover and chill in the refrigerator for about 30 minutes.

2 Preheat the oven to 180°C/350°F/Gas 4. Open out the sheets of filo pastry, keeping them in a pile so they do not dry out, and brush the top one with a little melted butter. Take lumps of the almond paste and roll them into fingers. Place them end to end along the long edge of the top sheet of filo, then roll the filo up into a roll the thickness of your thumb, tucking in the ends to stop the filling oozing out. Repeat with the other sheets of filo, until all the filling is used up.

3 Grease a large round baking pan or the widest baking sheet you can find. Lift one of the filo rolls in both hands and gently push it together from both ends, like an accordion, to relax the pastry before coiling it in the centre of the pan or baking sheet. Do the same with the other rolls, placing them end to end to form a tight coil like a snake.

4 Mix the egg yolk with a little water and brush this over the pastry, then bake for 30–35 minutes, until crisp and lightly browned. Top with a liberal sprinkling of icing sugar, and add lines of cinnamon like the spokes of a wheel. Serve at room temperature.

The snake, or m'hanncha *as it is known in Arabic, is the most famous, traditional sweet dish in Morocco. This coiled pastry looks impressive and tastes divine. The crisp, buttery filo is filled with almond paste that has been scented with cinnamon and orange flower water.*

Mint Tea

Serves 2

10ml/2 tsp Chinese gunpowder
    green tea
small bunch of fresh mint leaves
sugar, to taste

Known as atay bi nahna, *this is the national drink of Morocco, drunk in the morning, offered throughout the day while bargaining, conducting business, or wandering about, and served at the end of a meal to aid digestion. A blend of Chinese gunpowder green tea and fresh mint, traditionally sweetened with at least four sugar lumps per cup or glass, it is incredibly refreshing on a hot day.*

1 Put the tea in small pot and fill with boiling water. Add the mint leaves and leave it to infuse (steep) for 2–3 minutes. Stir in sugar to taste and pour into tea glasses or cups.

SERVING MINT TEA

At feasts and on special occasions, the making of mint tea can be an elaborate ceremony: the best green tea is chosen and only fresh spearmint (*Mentha spicata*), of which a well-known cultivar called Moroccan is used. A fine silver-plated, bulbous-shaped teapot is selected for brewing and the heavily sweetened tea is poured rhythmically into fine glasses. For an additional flounce of ceremony, a fresh, fragrant orange blossom or jasmine flower may be floated in each glass. In winter, wormwood is sometimes added for extra warmth, and infusions flavoured with aniseed or verbena are quite common.

Nutritional notes

Bissara Dip with Zahtar: Energy 320kcal/1343kJ; Protein 23.8g; Carbohydrate 29.5g, of which sugars 5.3g; Fat 13.3g, of which saturates 1.9g; Cholesterol 0mg; Calcium 113mg; Fibre 32.6g; Sodium 14mg.

Honey-spiced Artichoke Hearts: Energy 142kcal/586kJ; Protein 1.6g; Carbohydrate 4.1g, of which sugars 1.9g; Fat 11.3g, of which saturates 1.6g; Cholesterol 0mg; Calcium 40mg; Fibre 1.6g; Sodium 47mg.

Grilled Auberine: Energy 151kcal/631kJ; Protein 1.4g; Carbohydrate 17.6g, of which sugars 17.3g; Fat 8.9g, of which saturates 1.3g; Cholesterol 0mg; Calcium 16mg; Fibre 3g; Sodium 5mg.

Feta Cheese Cigars: Energy 105kcal/437kJ; Protein 3.6g; Carbohydrate 3.9g, of which sugars 0.3g; Fat 8.4g, of which saturates 2.7g; Cholesterol 39mg; Calcium 65mg; Fibre 0.2g; Sodium 213mg.

Chunky Tomato Soup: Energy 367kcal/1549kJ; Protein 10.6g; Carbohydrate 60.8g, of which sugars 22.7g; Fat 10.9g, of which saturates 1.5g; Cholesterol 0mg; Calcium 166mg; Fibre 11.3g; Sodium 490mg.

Sesame-coated Majoun: Energy 409kcal/1704kJ; Protein 8.3g; Carbohydrate 29.1g, of which sugars 28.3g; Fat 29.7g, of which saturates 5.7g; Cholesterol 14mg; Calcium 105mg; Fibre 1.6g; Sodium 61mg.

Pan-fried Baby Squid with Spices: Energy 154kcal/647kJ; Protein 19.8g; Carbohydrate 5.8g, of which sugars 4.3g; Fat 5.9g, of which saturates 1g; Cholesterol 281mg; Calcium 54mg; Fibre 1g; Sodium 144mg.

Bus-station Kefta: Energy 351kcal/1463kJ; Protein 23.3g; Carbohydrate 16.1g, of which sugars 5.9g; Fat 21.9g, of which saturates 6.6g; Cholesterol 332mg; Calcium 112mg; Fibre 2.6g; Sodium 283mg.

Casablancan Couscous: Energy 561kcal/2340kJ; Protein 10.4g; Carbohydrate 78.8g, of which sugars 18.7g; Fat 24.6g, of which saturates 3.5g; Cholesterol 0mg; Calcium 101mg; Fibre 7.2g; Sodium 51mg.

Spicy Couscous with Aromatic Shellfish Broth: Energy 338kcal/1422kJ; Protein 33.7g; Carbohydrate 24.7g, of which sugars 12.1g; Fat 12.4g, of which saturates 1.8g; Cholesterol 23mg; Calcium 100mg; Fibre 6.6g; Sodium 517mg.

Tagine of Lamb with Crunchy Country Salad: Energy 600kcal/2504kJ; Protein 42g; Carbohydrate 28.2g, of which sugars 25.8g; Fat 36.3g, of which saturates 10.9g; Cholesterol 222mg; Calcium 112mg; Fibre 4.9g; Sodium 199mg.

Tagine of Artichoke Hearts, Potatoes, Peas and Saffron: Energy 359kcal/1509kJ; Protein 13.9g; Carbohydrate 45g, of which sugars 19.3g; Fat 15g, of which saturates 2.1g; Cholesterol 0mg; Calcium 123mg; Fibre 9.7g; Sodium 597mg.

Tagine of Monkfish, Potatoes, Cherry Tomatoes and Olives: Energy 411kcal/1727kJ; Protein 41.2g; Carbohydrate 13.7g, of which sugars 3.9g, Fat 21.8g, of which saturates 2.1g; Cholesterol 60mg; Calcium 143mg; Fibre 4.3g; Sodium 821mg.

Tagine of Spiced Kefta: Energy 344kcal/1436kJ; Protein 21.6g; Carbohydrate 15.3g, of which sugars 5.3g; Fat 22.5g, of which saturates 7.5g; Cholesterol 286mg; Calcium 103mg; Fibre 1.8g; Sodium 280mg.

Summer Vegetable Kebabs: Energy 274kcal/1144kJ; Protein 11.1g; Carbohydrate 28.8g, of which sugars 26.2g; Fat 13.7g, of which saturates 2.5g; Cholesterol 1mg; Calcium 303mg; Fibre 5.9g; Sodium 111mg.

Spiced Sardines with Grapefruit and Fennel Salad: Energy 274kcal/1142kJ; Protein 18.7g; Carbohydrate 7.3g, of which sugars 6.1g; Fat 19.2g, of which saturates 3.9g; Cholesterol 0mg; Calcium 106mg; Fibre 2.3g; Sodium 109mg

Fiery Chicken Wings: Energy 243kcal/1007kJ; Protein 20g; Carbohydrate 1g, of which sugars 0g; Fat 18g, of which saturates 4g; Cholesterol 100mg; Calcium 11mg; Fibre 0g; Sodium 562mg.

Spicy Minced Beef Kebabs: Energy 456kcal/1898kJ; Protein 26.6g; Carbohydrate 21.8g, of which sugars 3.5g; Fat 29.8g, of which saturates 10.7g; Cholesterol 64mg; Calcium 153mg; Fibre 5.4g; Sodium 463mg.

Beetroot Salad: Energy 58kcal/247kJ; Protein 2.2g; Carbohydrate 12.9g, of which sugars 12.2g; Fat 0.1g, of which saturates 0g; Cholesterol 0mg; Calcium 33mg; Fibre 2.5g; Sodium 75mg

Sautéed Herb Salad: Energy 142kcal/585kJ; Protein 3.6g; Carbohydrate 3.1g, of which sugars 2.7g; Fat 12.9g, of which saturates 2.1g; Cholesterol 2mg; Calcium 216mg; Fibre 4.4g; Sodium 82mg.

Broad Bean Salad: Energy 272kcal/1143kJ; Protein 16.6g; Carbohydrate 24.6g, of which sugars 2.9g; Fat 12.7g, of which saturates 1.8g; Cholesterol 0mg; Calcium 142mg; Fibre 13.6g; Sodium 21mg.

Carrot Salad: Energy 53kcal/220kJ; Protein 0.6g; Carbohydrate 4.2g, of which sugars 3.9g; Fat 3.9g, of which saturates 0.6g; Cholesterol 0mg; Calcium 29mg; Fibre 1.6g; Sodium 15mg

Pomegranate Yogurt with Grapefruit Salad: Energy 188kcal/784kJ; Protein 8.8g; Carbohydrate 18g, of which sugars 18g; Fat 10.5g, of which saturates 5.2g; Cholesterol 0mg; Calcium 202mg; Fibre 3.6g; Sodium 82mg

Poached Pears: Energy 105kcal447kJ; Protein 1g; Carbohydrate 27g, of which sugars 27g; Fat 0g, of which saturates 0g; Cholesterol 0mg; Calcium 117mg; Fibre 3.2g; Sodium 6mg.

Burnt Mulhalbia: Energy 282kcal/1195kJ; Protein 8.3g; Carbohydrate 56.4g, of which sugars 46.4g; Fat 3.7g, of which saturates 2.5g; Cholesterol 16mg; Calcium 254mg; Fibre 0.3g; Sodium 118mg.

Yogurt Cake: Energy 152kcal/638kJ; Protein 6.6g; Carbohydrate 16g, of which sugars 14.1g; Fat 7.9g, of which saturates 3.4g; Cholesterol 95mg; Calcium 99mg; Fibre 0.1g; Sodium 71mg.

M'hanncha: Energy 366kcal/1523kJ; Protein 9g; Carbohydrate 20g, of which sugars 8g; Fat 28g, of which saturates 8g; Cholesterol 81mg; Calcium 82mg; Fibre 4g; Sodium 92mg.

Index